WILLIAM CATHERINE

TO COMMEMORATE THE MARRIAGE OF PRINCE WILLIAM OF WALES
AND MISS CATHERINE MIDDLETON, 29 APRIL 2011

WILLIAM &
CATHERINE

A ROYAL WEDDING SOUVENIR

ANNIE BULLEN

PITKIN

· GUIDES ·

Front cover: Prince William, Duke of Cambridge and Catherine, Duchess of Cambridge stand together smiling outside the Great West Door of Westminster Abbey following their wedding on Friday 29 April 2011.
Back cover: William and Catherine leave the afternoon reception at Buckingham Palace in a decorated vintage Aston Martin.

Frontispiece: The newly-weds kiss on the balcony of Buckingham Palace.
Title pages: Catherine's engagement and wedding rings.
Prince William and Catherine share a joyful glance as they are driven by carriage to Buckingham Palace after their wedding.
Opposite: Prince William places the wedding ring, made from Welsh gold, on to his bride's finger.

Written by Annie Bullen.
The moral right of the author has been asserted.

The author would like to thank Brian Hoey for information used from his book *Prince William*.

Editorial consultant Brian Hoey. The publisher would like to thank Brian Hoey for writing the Foreword and for his editorial guidance.

Edited by Shelley Grimwood and Gill Knappett.
Picture research by Jan Kean.
Cover designed by Katie Beard.
Designed by Glad Stockdale.
Production by Karen Kinnear.

A CIP catalogue record for this book is available from the British Library.
Published by Pitkin Publishing, Healey House, Dene Road, Andover, Hampshire, SP10 2AA.
www.pitkin-guides.com

Printed in Great Britain.
ISBN 978-1-84165-358-7   1/11

CONTENTS

A ROYAL *Love Story*

On Friday 29 April we witnessed the wedding of the decade, celebrated by an outpouring of national joy and an international feeling of genuine affection for the happy couple. Together, Prince William the Duke of Cambridge and Catherine, the Duchess, known to the world until her marriage as Kate Middleton, are perfect examples of a young generation that proves one's origins do not matter when love is involved.

The Middletons could be described as the face of modern Britain: hard-working, self-made and entrepreneurial – a middle-class family who have successfully bridged the gap between their modest origins and royalty.

William and Catherine are the products of prestigious public schools – Eton and Marlborough – and an equally exclusive university, St Andrews. They have not rushed into marriage; their love has blossomed out of a feeling of true companionship and they share many interests, enjoying a mutual understanding that is the basis for every successful relationship. They are not just in love, they are also the best of friends.

The couple have captured the public's attention in a way not seen since William's mother, the late Diana, Princess of Wales, arrived on the royal scene in 1981. They have accomplished this is in complete contrast to the former reverential image of royalty, when the mere mention of their names would have been in hushed tones.

Today, William, with his boyish good looks, undoubted charm and self-deprecating sense of humour, and Catherine, whose natural beauty and outgoing personality make her a photographer's dream, generate an impression of royalty that is a formidable combination of star quality and an approachable common touch.

William's life has been mapped out from the moment he was born. He is a king-in-waiting, and his education and subsequent career to date have been part of his ongoing training as a future monarch. He accepts this as an inevitable part of his destiny. It is the job for which he will be best qualified and for which he is the only applicant. As The Queen's grandson, he displays that Windsor streak of strong self-discipline when it is needed. He may be considered to be one of the most informal royals of recent years; however, if and when the occasion demands it, he can be as traditional and conventional as every other member of the most famous family in the world. Nevertheless, William has been more fortunate than previous princes in his position in that he has enjoyed much more freedom and he has been able to develop an independence formerly unknown among royalty.

The new Duchess's different background is seen as a definite advantage. She comes from a stable family who have welcomed Prince William to their home and, he says, given him a glimpse of the kind of happiness he hopes to share in the years to come. Catherine brings into the Royal Family grace and dignity along with her beauty and intelligence. William recognized these qualities the first time they met and he says that one of the things he finds so appealing and attractive in Catherine is their shared sense of humour.

William likes his life to be ordered and planned – he has never known anything else – and his wife will need to become used to the formality accepted as normal by generations of royalty. The couple are the new, modern face of royalty. Together they will ensure the continued stability of the monarchy when the time comes for Prince William to ascend the throne. They both understand the responsibilities they will be required to bear.

Above: William and Catherine share a tender glance as they prepare to walk down the aisle.

Catherine's introduction to life as a member of the Royal Family will be carried out with the utmost care and consideration, so that she may move seamlessly into the role she will play within 'The Firm' – the name King George VI bestowed on the immediate Royal Family over 60 years ago. As a duchess, Catherine will be required to undertake public duties, but her prime responsibility in the early years will be as wife to a serving officer in the Royal Air Force. By happy coincidence, their first foreign tour as a married couple will be to Canada in the summer of 2011. William knows the country well and the Royal Family is very popular there, The Queen having made frequent visits. So it will be a gentle introduction. Nevertheless, for the new royal bride this will mean unending attention to her choice of outfits, her every move and her demeanour.

There is a groundswell of public goodwill towards William and his wife that should continue to encourage them as they begin married life. The royal wedding was a cause for celebration and the couple were delighted that so many people joined in the festivities and shared their happiness. The Duke and Duchess are the stars of the future, the jewels in the royal crown. Together they are a priceless asset of the Royal Family and the country. They know that the course of their lives for the foreseeable future will follow a pre-arranged path, and that some time this century they will be King and Queen Consort of the United Kingdom. They both understand how important it is for them to be ready for that day. And, if they are looking for an object lesson in how to achieve their aims, they can do no better than to follow the flawless example set by William's grandmother, Her Majesty The Queen.

May they have a long, happy and successful marriage.

Brian Hoey

DATES & EVENTS

1982   Catherine Middleton and Prince William were born; Miss Middleton at the Royal Berkshire Hospital, Reading, Berkshire, on 9 January, the Prince on 21 June at the private Lindo Wing of St Mary's Hospital, Paddington, London.

1985   William's first day at school; the decision to send him to a nursery school broke with royal tradition.

1991   The young Prince William undertakes an early public engagement when he accompanies his parents, Prince Charles and Princess Diana, on a visit to Llandaff Cathedral to celebrate St David's Day.

1995   Prince William, as 'William Wales', goes to Eton College, in Berkshire. Catherine Middleton is a pupil at Marlborough College, in Wiltshire.

2000–01 Both William and Catherine opt for 'gap years' before university. Although they did not meet, Catherine worked at a project in Chile in 2001 where Prince William had been a month earlier.

2001   William and Catherine meet at St Andrews University, where they are both studying Art History; they have rooms close to each other in St Salvator's Hall.

2002   In March, William buys a £200 ticket to a charity fashion show and is impressed by Catherine's appearance on the catwalk.

2002   In September, they move into a student flat in Hope Street, St Andrews, with two other friends.

2003   In May, newspapers publish photographs of William and Catherine deep in conversation at a rugby match.

2003   Catherine is a guest at William's 21st birthday party at Windsor Castle; in September, they move into a cottage, for their third year at university.

2004   The couple are pictured together on the ski slopes at Klosters, Switzerland.

2005   In June, Catherine joins William for the wedding of his friend Hugh van Cutsem; the couple graduate from St Andrews.

2005   The couple fly to Kenya for a holiday at the Lewa Downs game reserve.

2006   Prince William is photographed for the first time kissing Catherine, during another skiing holiday at Klosters in January.

2006   In January, Prince William starts his army training at Sandhurst.

2006   In May, Catherine is invited to the wedding of Laura Parker Bowles, the Prince's stepsister.

2006 In November, Catherine begins work as an accessories buyer for fashion chain Jigsaw.

2006 In December, Catherine is invited to Sandhurst to watch William graduate as an army officer.

2007 Prince William starts army training in Dorset. In March, William and Catherine are photographed together watching the Cheltenham Gold Cup.

2007 In April, it is confirmed that William and Catherine have split up; by June there are rumours that they are back together again.

2007 In October, they are photographed out on the town together and Catherine is invited to Balmoral for the weekend.

2008 In April, Catherine is at the Prince's side as he graduates from the RAF at Cranwell.

2008 In June, for the first time Catherine appears at a formal royal public occasion to watch William taking part in the Order of the Garter Service at Windsor Castle.

2008 William and Catherine enjoy a holiday at Birkhall, the Prince of Wales's private hunting lodge on the Balmoral estate, in Scotland.

2009 In May, the couple are photographed together at a polo match.

2010 William and Catherine take a New Year break at Birkhall.

2010 In January, Catherine watches as William graduates from an advanced helicopter flying course, receiving his wings from his father, the Prince of Wales.

2010 In March, the couple join Catherine's parents on holiday in Courchevel, France.

2010 On 16 November a brief statement is released from Clarence House announcing William and Catherine's engagement. A week later Westminster Abbey is chosen as the church for the wedding on 29 April 2011.

2011 In February, William is made a Colonel in the Irish Guards. Catherine attends her first official engagements with her fiancé, naming a new lifeboat in Anglesey. The following day, at the University of St Andrews, where they met, they mark the Prince's appointment as patron of the university's 600th anniversary appeal.

2011 In March, the couple make an official visit to Northern Ireland. A week later, the Prince pays an official visit to Australia and New Zealand.

2011 On 29 April, William and Catherine marry at Westminster Abbey.

THE ROYAL
Wedding

Catherine Middleton, a radiant and beautiful bride, her hand clasped firmly in her father's, stood for a few seconds in the light-filled space just inside the Great West Door of Westminster Abbey. Ahead stretched a crimson carpet marking the length of the nave and the quire to the sanctuary, where her bridegroom, Prince William, resplendent in his scarlet uniform of Colonel of the Irish guards, waited for her. Behind, outside the magnificent Abbey, were almost a million well-wishers, filling the parks and streets in their quest to be part of the royal love story that has moved so many.

Catherine's transformation from commoner to Duchess, from single woman to wife, began as she started the long walk down the nave, led by the Very Reverend Dr John Hall, Dean of Westminster, to stand at Prince William's side. The choir sang the soaring anthem *I Was Glad*, written by Charles Hubert Hastings Parry from Psalm 122, as the bride processed slowly to the High Altar.

Above: Catherine waves as she travels to Westminster Abbey with her father, Michael Middleton, in a Rolls Royce Phantom VI.

Above: Catherine, smiling behind her veil, prepares to enter Westminster Abbey.

Around the bride, her father, Michael Middleton, and her attendants, were almost 2,000 guests, all of whom would have been moved by her understated grace and beauty. Westminster Abbey, with its sweeping arches, the highest Gothic nave in the country, and a royal connection stretching back to the 11th century, is a glorious building at any time – on this occasion it was filled with a romance and magic that will have touched every guest.

A fresh green avenue of tall trees – field maples and hornbeams – and informal arrangements of cool white spring flowers along the nave and around the High Altar, gave a pastoral feeling, tempering the high majesty of the occasion. And as Catherine moved between them, towards her place on Prince William's left-hand side, the best man, Prince Harry, turned to watch her approach. As she reached his side, her bridegroom gazed at her and whispered, 'You look beautiful.'

The bridegroom and best man

The guests invited to the royal wedding were already lining up in a well-manned and beautifully dressed queue as the Great North Door of Westminster Abbey was ceremoniously opened, early on the morning of the wedding.

Outside the Abbey those without an invitation filled every available space along the route from Clarence House, Buckingham Palace and the Goring Hotel. They came from all walks of life, families and groups of friends, young and old, all with the sincere intent to let the young couple know how much they cared. Some dressed as brides or wore outfits ingeniously constructed from Union flags. Many had fantastic hats, and just about everyone waved the Union Jack on this most British of occasions.

Above: Prince William and his best man and brother, Prince Harry, are happy and at ease as they enter Westminster Abbey.

Left: The magnificent West Front of Westminster Abbey, at the heart of the royal wedding celebrations.

Bands of the Coldstream Guards, the Grenadier Guards, the Scots Guards, the Royal Marines, the Band of the Welsh Guards and the Central Band of the RAF added to the atmosphere as they marched and played to entertain the crowds. As the minutes ticked by, excitement mounted. Celebrities including David and Victoria Beckham, Rowan Atkinson and Sir Elton John arrived. Governors-General and Prime Ministers were escorted to their seats.

Guests paused in the doorway to gaze at the great sweep of red carpet, flowing around and past the poppy-encircled black marble Tomb of the Unknown Warrior, down through the Quire Screen to the intimate space before the High Altar, where the couple would make their vows to each other. All gasped at the avenue of trees which sat perfectly within the soaring arches of the ancient Abbey, and admired the banks of white and cream flowers that filled the spaces around the altar.

As the congregation settled into their seats, there was a sudden burst of cheering and a buzz of excitement from the onlookers outside. A claret-coloured Bentley had drawn up outside the Abbey, bearing the bridegroom, William, newly-made Duke of Cambridge, and his best man, Prince Harry. The brothers – William, his Garter Sash a vivid blue across his scarlet tunic which also bore his RAF Wings, the Garter Star and Golden Jubilee Medal, and Harry, wearing his formal Blues and Royals officer's uniform – were greeted by the Dean of Westminster.

The Royal Family and the bride's family

As the bridegroom and his best man made their way into the Abbey, Prince William stopped to greet friends. He and Harry exchanged a few words with their uncle, Charles Spencer, the ninth Earl Spencer, brother of their late mother, Princess Diana. Then the princes were escorted to the private space of St Edmund's Chapel to await the arrival of the bride.

The Dean was at the Great West Door, waiting to greet the parents of the bride and bridegroom. Carole Middleton – wearing a stunning, understated Catherine Walker knee-length, pale blue silk dress with pleated short sleeves, worn under a blue wool crêpe coat with satin piping and braid trim at the waist and cuff – arrived first, accompanied by her 23-year-old son, James.

HRH Prince Charles and his wife, the Duchess of Cornwall, stepped out of a 1950 Rolls Royce Phantom, she wearing a champagne silk dress designed by Anna Valentine with a matching champagne and duck-egg blue hand-embroidered coat.

The bridegroom's grandparents, Her Majesty The Queen and Prince Philip, were the last members of the Royal Family to arrive, following the others in a crowd-lined route that took them along The Mall, Horse Guards Road, Horse Guards Parade, through Horse Guards Arch (where they took a salute from a mounted Guard of Honour), along Whitehall, past Downing Street and the Cenotaph, through Parliament Square and along Broad Sanctuary to the Great West Door of the Abbey. Every inch of pavement space along the route was occupied by cheering, flag-waving crowds.

Above: The Queen and Prince Philip are greeted by the Very Reverend Dr John Hall, Dean of Westminster, as they arrive for the wedding of their grandson.

Above: Prince Charles, Prince of Wales, wearing naval officer's uniform with Garter Star and Medals, and Camilla, Duchess of Cornwall arrive at Westminster Abbey for the marriage of Prince William to Catherine Middleton.

Above: Carole Middleton, the proud and happy mother of the bride, turns to smile and wave as she arrives at Westminster Abbey for her daughter's wedding.

Her Majesty's primrose yellow single crêpe wool dress with hand-sewn beading at the neck in the shape of sunrays, worn underneath a matching tailored coat, was a cheerful spot of colour in an Abbey already full of bright outfits. Her designer, Angela Kelly, was responsible, too, for her matching hat that was trimmed with handmade silk roses and apricot-coloured leaves, following the natural theme of the ceremony. The Queen's True Lovers Knot diamond brooch once belonged to her grandmother, Queen Mary.

As The Queen and Prince Philip, who was dressed in the scarlet tunic of the Grenadier Guards, were greeted by the Dean, the Very Reverend Dr John Hall, a fanfare by the State Trumpeters of the Household Cavalry rang out, to announce Her Majesty's arrival. The stirring notes of Parry's *March from The Birds* was played by the London Chamber Orchestra as The Queen and Prince Philip, the Duchess of Cornwall and the Prince of Wales processed to their seats led by the Dean's verger and the Dean.

The ceremony

The hushed expectation, both inside the Abbey and outside, seemed almost too much to bear as the Rolls Royce Phantom VI carrying Catherine and her father drew to a precise halt outside the entrance to the great church. As the bride stepped from the wedding car, her sister and maid of honour, Philippa (Pippa), gathered the train of the exquisite bridal gown, while the small bridesmaids and pageboys clustered around, preparing Catherine for the long walk down the aisle that would change her life.

Above: The bride, her father and attendants, led by the Dean of Westminster, process slowly up the aisle to the High Altar where Prince William was waiting.

Catherine followed the tradition adopted by many brides of declining to vow obedience to her husband. As the couple made their promises to each other before the High Altar at Westminster Abbey, she pledged to love, comfort, honour and keep him.

Left: William and Catherine make their wedding vows before the Archbishop of Canterbury, Dr Rowan Williams.

As she and her father, whose hand she held, waited briefly for the procession to start to the exultant strains of Parry's Coronation anthem *I Was Glad,* the guests were quiet and still. The solemnity of the pageantry, and the majestic place in which they were gathered to witness this wedding, was tempered by anticipation and expectation. And as Catherine Middleton walked slowly, smiling a little, that anticipation was rewarded. She was beautiful and her dress, which had remained a secret until this moment, was perfect.

Pippa allowed her sister's train to fall naturally and walked behind the bride and her father, holding the hands of the two youngest bridesmaids, three-year-old Grace van Cutsem, Prince William's god-daughter, and Eliza Lopes, also three, granddaughter of the Duchess of Cornwall.

Then came Lady Louise Windsor, seven, daughter of the Earl and Countess of Wessex and Prince William's cousin, with the Hon. Margarita Armstrong-Jones, eight, daughter of Viscount and Viscountess Linley. Two young pageboys, Billy Lowther-Pinkerton, ten, son of Prince William's private secretary, and Tom Pettifer, the eight-year-old son of his former nanny, brought up the rear.

Prince William, waiting for his bride, turned towards her only as she arrived at his side. He complimented her and jokingly whispered to Michael Middleton, 'And this was supposed to be a small family affair.'

The two young stars of this wedding stood on the same spot where the coffin of Princess Diana had rested before the High Altar in 1997. This time, catharsis and a sense of healing must have struck her sons, William and Harry, even as the 1,900-strong congregation sang the same hymn, *Guide Me, O Thou Great Redeemer,* that featured at her funeral service. But this was a joyful rendering, mending the past and looking forward to a bright future.

The couple stepped up together to the sacrarium where, prompted by the Archbishop of Canterbury, the Most Reverend and Right Honourable Dr Rowan Williams, they made their vows, clearly and evenly. There was a collective sigh of relief as William, after a short struggle, slipped the wedding ring, made from Welsh gold, on to his bride's finger. All the while the cheers of those watching on large screens outside the Abbey rang out.

If the intention behind the ceremony, the service, the decorations and the wedding clothes was to demonstrate Britishness at its best, the couple and their advisors succeeded with a brilliance evident from start to finish.

The service was traditional, conforming to the Church of England's 1966 Book of Common Prayer. The Lord Bishop of London, the Right Reverend and Right Honourable Dr Richard Chartres, a clergyman who has known William since he was a child, gave the address, telling them 'Be who God meant you to be and you will set the world on fire' – words of the bride's namesake, St Catherine of Sienna, whose feast day is also celebrated on 29 April. He also revealed a prayer that William and Catherine had written together in preparation for their wedding day.

The sole reading was the Lesson, given by Catherine's younger brother, James, who delivered the advice from Romans 12 in a clear, steady voice. The passage contained the words: *Live in harmony with one another; do not be haughty, but associate with the lowly; do not claim to be wiser than you are.*

The only private moment for the couple and their families came as they moved to the chapel of St Edward the Confessor, built to honour the founder of Westminster Abbey, and containing his tomb. Here, in the presence of family witnesses, they signed the registers confirming their new status as man and wife. And here they might have said a quiet prayer to St Edward himself, a holy man, said to have had the power to heal.

The newly made Duchess of Cambridge bowed to her grandmother-in-law The Queen, before walking joyfully back down the aisle, hand-in-hand with her husband, the Duke. Guests stood and smiled to see the happiness of the young couple, and the Abbey bells rang out in splendid voice as they emerged into the spring sunshine to be greeted by the approving roar of a million well-wishers.

Above: Good wishes come from all sides as Prince William and his new wife, Catherine, walk together down the aisle after their wedding.

Above: William and Catherine leave Westminster Abbey after their marriage.

The music, chosen by Catherine and William with help from Prince Charles, showcased British composers. Pieces by Victorian composer Sir Charles Parry featured, as did music from William Walton, Sir Peter Maxwell Davies and a specially commissioned anthem from John Rutter. Young Welsh composer Paul Mealor wrote the motet *Ubi caritas et amor*, sung after the address. The service was sung by the choirs of Westminster Abbey and Her Majesty's Chapel Royal, conducted by the Abbey's organist and choirmaster James O'Donnell. Sub-organist Robert Quinney played during the service.

The wedding dress

The perfect ivory lace and satin dress, revealed to the world as Catherine Middleton stepped out of her wedding car, exceeded the expectations of the fashion critics. The lace and satin looked deliciously simple, but a world of craftsmanship, design, expertise and sheer genius had gone into its making by a team of expert needleworkers and dressmakers led by designer Sarah Burton, of Alexander McQueen, the British fashion house.

Sarah Burton's designs pay tribute to the British Arts and Crafts movement with an emphasis on fine materials and expert craftsmanship used to make the simple beautiful, often with a Romantic decorative style. On this occasion, her design involved the incorporation of appliquéd English and Chantilly (French) lace, hand-cut and stitched on to the dress and the train, using the Carrickmacross lacemaking technique, pioneered in Ireland almost 200 years ago. Each piece of lace was cut in the shape of a flower – the English rose, Scottish thistle, Welsh daffodil and Irish shamrock – before tiny stitches fastened them to the delicate fabric.

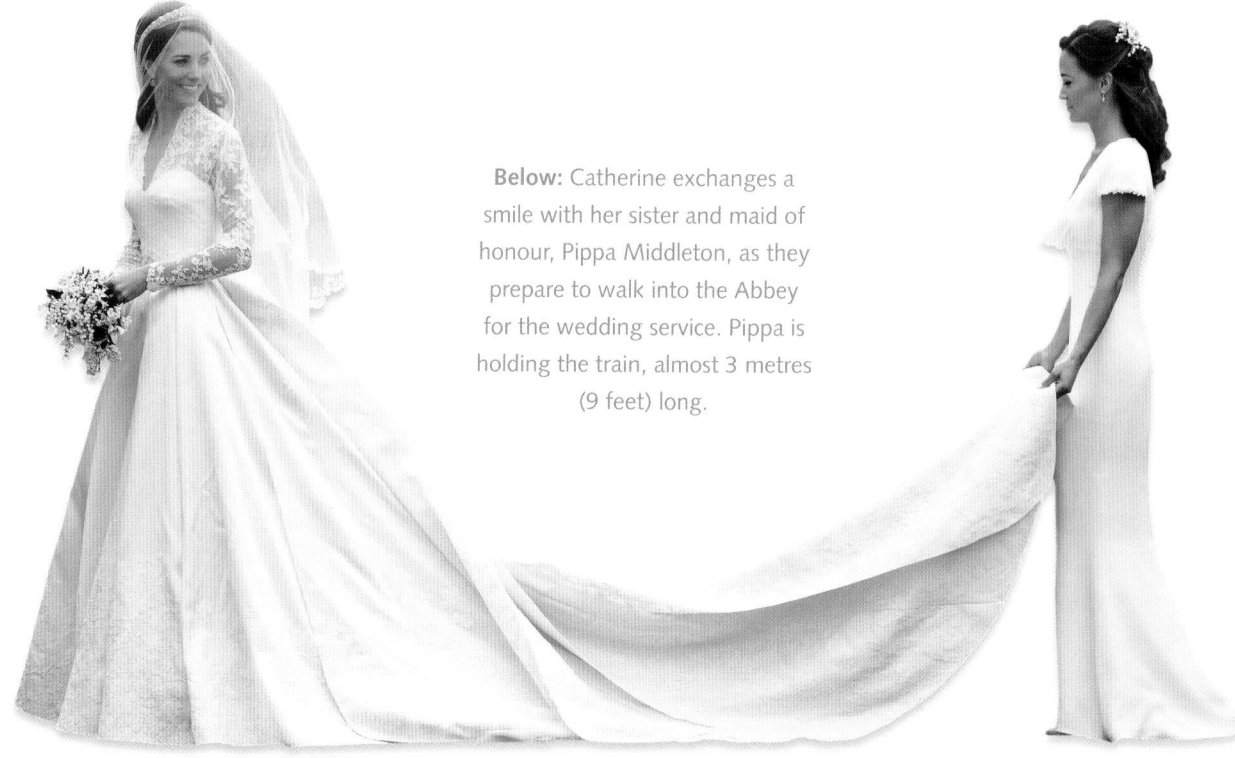

Below: Catherine exchanges a smile with her sister and maid of honour, Pippa Middleton, as they prepare to walk into the Abbey for the wedding service. Pippa is holding the train, almost 3 metres (9 feet) long.

Catherine's soft ivory silk tulle bridal veil, decorated with hand-embroidered flowers, was held in place by a Cartier 'halo' tiara, loaned to the bride by The Queen. It was made in 1936 and bought by Her Majesty's father, then the Duke of York, for his young wife, later Queen Elizabeth the Queen Mother. Some years later the tiara was given to the then Princess Elizabeth to celebrate her 18th birthday. Catherine's earrings were a wedding present from her parents, who commissioned a design based on their new family crest, incorporating diamond-set stylized oak leaves and acorns.

The skirt, of ivory and white satin gazar, evoked an opening flower, with a bodice of ivory satin finished at the back with 58 tiny satin-covered buttons. The silk tulle underskirt was trimmed with English Cluny lace. The stunning, yet modest, dress with its slender lace sleeves, decorous neckline and glorious swagged train was perfectly suited to Catherine's serene nature. Fashion experts have compared her quiet style to that of another royal bride – the late Grace Kelly, who married Prince Rainier of Monaco in April 1956.

Workers at the Royal School of Needlework, based at Hampton Court Palace, cut out delicate flower motifs from the lace fabrics of Catherine's wedding dress. They positioned the lace roses, thistles, daffodils and shamrocks on to the train and skirt, the bodice and sleeves, veil, and even the shoes, before stitching them on with absolute precision. They washed their hands every half-hour and renewed their needles every three hours to keep the fabrics and threads pristine.

Above: Pippa Middleton and dress designer Sarah Burton make last-minute adjustments to the gown as the bride and her father prepare for the walk along the aisle of Westminster Abbey.

Above: The bride's silk veil, held in place by a Cartier tiara owned by Her Majesty The Queen, was – like the dress – covered with hand-embroidered flowers. Her delicate earrings were a wedding present from her parents.

The bride's attendants

The four young bridesmaids will always be reminded of the parts they played on this momentous day, for embroidered into the lining of each of their handmade dresses is their name and the date of the wedding.

Lady Louise Windsor, the Hon. Margarita Armstrong-Jones, and the three-year-olds, Grace van Cutsem and Eliza Lopes, wore simple ballerina-length dresses with full skirts emphasized by layers of underskirt. They were made by children's-wear designer Nicki Macfarlane from the same materials used in Catherine's dress. Puff sleeves and the necklines were trimmed with lace, while the backs were finished with the same button detail used in the bride's dress. The sashes, tied at the back in an elaborate bow, were of pale gold, wild silk. Each of the younger attendants wore wreaths of lilies of the valley and ivy in her hair, and all carried small bouquets of flowers which matched those of the bride.

The pageboys' uniforms were inspired by the style of those worn by a Foot Guards officer in 1820, during the Regency. The young boys, Billy Lowther-Pinkerton and Tom Pettifer, wore Guards' Red tunics with gold piping, Irish shamrocks on the collars, and buttons featuring the Harp of Ireland. The insignia on the tunics was influenced by that of the Irish Guards, whose Colonel is Prince William. The pages wore ivory breeches with white stockings and black buckled shoes. Their gold and crimson tasselled sashes were modelled on those worn by Irish Guards officers when in the presence of a member of the Royal Family.

The only adult attendant, Catherine's sister, Pippa, looked stunning in a dress created, like that of her sister, by Sarah Burton, of Alexander McQueen. It was of heavy ivory satin-based crêpe with a cowl front and the same button and lace detail as Catherine's gown.

Above: The attendants – Lady Louise Windsor, the Hon. Margarita Armstrong-Jones, Tom Pettifer and William Lowther-Pinkerton – laugh together as they arrive at Westminster Abbey.

Above: Maid of honour Pippa Middleton, sister of the bride, holds hands with the two small bridesmaids, Grace van Cutsem and Eliza Lopes.

Pippa Middleton, Catherine's younger sister and maid of honour, kept a close eye on the two younger bridesmaids, holding them by the hand as they walked down the aisle. And Prince Harry, who looked after three of the young attendants on the carriage drive back to Buckingham Palace, brought with him a tiny 'wiggly worm' toy to keep them amused. Three-year-old Eliza Lopes, granddaughter to Harry's stepmother, Camilla, Duchess of Cornwall, liked the toy so much she kept it clasped firmly in her hand – even in the official photographs taken in Buckingham Palace Throne Room.

The carriage procession

The radiance and the great happiness in the hearts of the newly-weds, and of all who watched and wished them well as they emerged from Westminster Abbey after the ceremony, was palpable. A real feeling of celebration and joy suffused the atmosphere.

As Catherine and William stepped out into the spring sunshine bathing the ancient stone of the Abbey, the bells pealing and the crowds roaring approval, their carriage, the gorgeous 1902 State Landau, resplendent with red leather, crimson satin and gold leaf, was waiting to transport them to Buckingham Palace. Catherine seemed, briefly, to be taken aback by the size of the one million-strong crowd, but she recovered her composure, to give practised royal waves quite in time with those of her new husband.

After the arrival of the wedding party at the Abbey by motor vehicles, however splendid, the five-strong carriage procession with its two mounted escorts was British pageantry at its best. The newly-weds were borne away, liveried coachmen riding on the back of the carriage and a mounted Captain's Escort of 24 troopers, 12 from the Lifeguards and another dozen Household Cavalry men, surrounding them. Following closely behind were two Ascot Landaus, one bearing Prince Harry and three attendants, and the other carrying Pippa Middleton accompanying the remaining three children.

A larger Sovereign's Escort, 50-strong, accompanied the 1830 Scottish State Coach, which carried The Queen and the Duke of Edinburgh back to the Palace. Taking up the rear was the carriage transporting the parents of the bride and bridegroom, the Prince of Wales and Duchess of Cornwall, and Carole and Michael Middleton.

As they passed into the historic tilt yard at Horse Guards, through the low arch that was once the entrance to the royal palaces, salutes were exchanged and the procession moved smartly on, into The Mall, before drawing up outside Buckingham Palace, where the Royal Standard fluttered aloft and 101 men from the 1st Battalion Welsh Guards formed a Guard of Honour.

Prince William had brought his bride safely home.

Above: Her Majesty The Queen and Prince Philip, Duke of Edinburgh are driven in the Scottish State Coach to Buckingham Palace, following the wedding service.

Above: Prince Harry and Lady Louise Windsor wave as they ride in the carriage procession after leaving the Abbey.

Above: Prince William holds his wife's wedding flowers as she is helped from the carriage by a footman on their arrival at Buckingham Palace.

Right: The splendid carriage procession carrying the wedding party from Westminster Abbey to The Queen's reception for the couple at Buckingham Palace was led by the 1902 State Landau which carried the bride and bridegroom through the cheering crowds. They travelled with a mounted Captain's Escort of 24 troopers.

Celebration and jubilation

The enthusiastic crowd, which had surged along The Mall, swept through the barriers to reach the palace railings, and waited for what has become a traditional highlight of any great royal occasion − the appearance of the Royal Family on Buckingham Palace's balcony. And what everyone wanted to see, above all, was that very public kiss by the bride and groom.

After much curtain-twitching and false hope, at last the doors opened and the newly-weds emerged, hand-in-hand, to wave to the thousands of well-wishers. Soon William and Catherine were joined by the rest of the wedding party: The Queen and the Duke of Edinburgh, Prince Charles and the Duchess of Cornwall, Prince Harry, Carole and Michael Middleton, their other daughter, Pippa, and their son, James, and the young bridesmaids and pageboys.

Then it came. Not a long, lingering kiss, but not a perfunctory peck either. And the crowd roared, hoping for another. They were not disappointed. The second kiss, when it came, was just that little bit more certain and won the same approval from the jubilant public.

Above: The newly married couple share a kiss on the balcony of Buckingham Palace.

Above: Well-wishers waving Union flags surge along The Mall towards Buckingham Palace to celebrate the royal wedding.

Left: It was party time as many communities came together in celebration of the royal wedding.

And, after a magnificent and ear-splitting fly-past by the Lancaster, Spitfire and Hurricane of the Battle of Britain Memorial Flight, it was all over, for the public at least. The Queen's reception at Buckingham Palace, for 650 wedding guests, followed the wedding party's appearance on the balcony. Guests tucked into Cornish crab salad and duck terrine, smoked salmon on beetroot blinis, quail eggs and asparagus spears, langoustines, pork belly and wedding cake, as they sipped champagne.

The newly-weds took a break between the afternoon and evening receptions, at Clarence House, Prince Charles's London residence – Prince William driving Catherine there in his father's 41-year-old dark blue convertible Aston Martin decorated with 'L' plates, balloons and ribbon, and a rear number plate that read 'JU5T WED'. The partying went on well into the night, as Prince Charles hosted a dinner dance for more than 300 guests at the Palace, and ended with a spectacular fireworks display.

As thousands of people around Britain celebrated the wedding of His Royal Highness Prince William of Wales KG and Miss Catherine Middleton – still fondly referred to by most as 'Wills and Kate', millions more around the world followed the ceremony and pageant of a perfect day on television. It has been estimated that one in every three people in the world will have seen the wedding.

Genuine goodwill and sincere wishes for a young couple clearly in love came from communities throughout Britain, many feeling that, in Catherine, Prince William has found a partner who will be his help and support when he eventually succeeds to the throne.

Back in Catherine's home village of Bucklebury, in Berkshire, there was general rejoicing and a party atmosphere heightened by traditional English activities, including Morris dancing, duck and sheep racing, beer drinking – and many small girls dressing up as princesses for the day.

Bucklebury's day of rejoicing was echoed around Britain, as neighbours celebrated in the street, garden parties got under way and people gathered together to watch the wedding and enjoy themselves at the same time.

It was a day that will be remembered for a glorious show of perfect British pageantry and pomp, though it will also remain with everyone as a family day when reserve broke down and spontaneity, friendship and love brought home the real meaning of a wedding.

Above: The wedding party gather in the Throne Room of Buckingham Palace with the bride and bridegroom, the Duke and Duchess of Cambridge. In the front row are: Grace van Cutsem, Eliza Lopes, HRH the Duke of Edinburgh, HM The Queen, the Hon. Margarita Armstrong-Jones, Lady Louise Windsor, William Lowther-Pinkerton. Back row: Tom Pettifer, HRH Camilla, Duchess of Cornwall, Prince Charles, HRH the Prince of Wales, HRH Prince Harry of Wales, Mr Michael Middleton, Mrs Carole Middleton, Mr James Middleton, Miss Pippa Middleton.

Above: The bride and bridegroom pose for an official photograph in the Throne Room of Buckingham Palace with (clockwise from bottom right) the Hon. Margarita Armstrong-Jones, Eliza Lopes, Grace van Cutsem, Lady Louise Windsor, Tom Pettifer and William Lowther-Pinkerton.

The couple started married life with three new titles each. In addition to the titles of Duke and Duchess of Cambridge, Her Majesty The Queen has made William Earl of Strathearn and Baron Carrickfergus. Catherine will, in turn, become Countess of Strathearn and Baroness Carrickfergus.

THE Engagement

The announcement from Clarence House, just after 11 o'clock on Tuesday 16 November 2010, was matter-of-fact, but its joyful impact was felt by a nation hungry for a genuine love story.

And there could be no doubt in anyone's mind that this was the real thing. Catherine Middleton took Prince William's arm as they walked into the red and gold grandeur of the Entrée Room at St James's Palace to face the world's media. Love shone through every gesture, each exchanged glance and every movement towards each other as the young couple, standing closely together under historic royal portraits, told of their happiness and their plans for the future.

And Catherine, facing her first formal public appearance with her royal fiancé, emerged with credit from this debut. She admitted that the prospect of joining the Royal Family was a daunting one.

'I hope I'll take it in my stride,' she said, turning towards the Prince. 'And William's a great teacher, so hopefully he'll be able to help me along the way.'

The Queen admitted her joy at the 'brilliant' news. Prince Charles, too, said he was thrilled and, in a characteristic display of dry humour, added: 'they've been practising long enough.' William's stepmother, the Duchess of Cornwall, was clearly delighted. She told reporters: 'I'm just so happy and so are they. It's wicked!'

William said he has grown very fond of Catherine's family. 'Kate's got a very, very close family. I get on really well with them and I'm very lucky that they've been so supportive. Mike and Carole have been really loving and caring and welcoming towards me, so I've felt really a part of the family.'

Left: Catherine's deep-sapphire blue dress was a perfect match for her engagement ring.

Above: A loving look passes between the happy couple as they tell
the world of their plans to marry.

When William and Catherine shared their happy news with a delighted world, her arm tucked through his as she leaned towards him, no one could have failed to notice the beautiful sapphire, surrounded by 14 brilliant cut diamonds, set in a white-gold band on the third finger of her perfectly manicured left hand.

Catherine's oval engagement ring, now one of the most famous gems in the world, is of huge sentimental value to Prince William and of more than usual emotional significance to the happy couple. It was the ring given to the Prince's mother, then Lady Diana Spencer, by Prince Charles when he proposed 29 years previously.

William, who inherited the ring from his mother's estate after her death in 1997, showed that it was priceless to him by choosing to present it to his fiancée as she accepted his proposal of marriage.

'It's very special to me,' William told the world as cameras homed in on the sparkling ring, which fitted Catherine perfectly without alteration. 'Kate is very special to me now as well, and it is only right that the two are put together. It was my way of making sure that my mother didn't miss out on today, and the excitement and the fact that we're going to spend the rest of our lives together.'

William revealed that he did actually ask Catherine's father, Michael Middleton, for his daughter's hand in marriage – but he waited until she had accepted his proposal.

'I was torn between asking Kate's father first and then the realization that he might actually say "no" dawned. So I thought, "If I ask Kate first, he can't really say no". So I did it that way.'

Left: Smiling for the cameras. The engagement was announced amid the grandeur of St James's Palace.

William is heir presumptive, second in line to the throne, Britain's future king, brought up with every privilege that accrues to royalty.

Catherine comes from a wealthy middle-class family, rather than from the elite aristocracy from whose circles William might have been expected to choose a bride.

His family background is understandably more formal, bound by duty, tradition and royal protocol. He lost his beloved mother in a tragic accident when he was just 15.

Her family is close-knit, her parents Carole and Michael giving Catherine and her siblings, Pippa and James, a happy and comfortable childhood in the Home Counties.

Both Prince William and Catherine had time over their long friendship and romance to get to know their prospective in-laws – a relationship more daunting for the bride-to-be than the Prince. But although Catherine admits that she was nervous about meeting Prince Charles, William's father, her fears were unfounded. She says that he was 'very, very welcoming, very friendly' and the meeting could not have gone more easily.

When Prince William and Catherine Middleton flew out to Kenya in October 2010, she had no idea that this was anything more than a three-week holiday to see spectacular wildlife and to enjoy some time together in the seclusion of the African bush.

But tucked away in William's rucksack was the symbol of his love, his late mother's sapphire and diamond ring, which he planned to put on Catherine's finger if she agreed to become his wife.

Just before their holiday was due to end, William drove Catherine to the beautiful shores of the Rutundu Lake, high on the slopes of Mount Kenya, where the couple stayed in a romantic wooden lodge overlooking beautiful scenery. It was here that the Prince asked Catherine to be his wife. And it was here that she accepted him and the pledge of his affection, the sapphire ring. Neither William nor Catherine revealed any details of the proposal. Catherine would only say: 'It was very romantic and it was very personal.'

Right: Catherine's engagement ring holds special memories: it was given to William's mother, Princess Diana, on her engagement to Prince Charles.

Left: Catherine's engagement ring is a beautiful sapphire, surrounded by 14 brilliant cut diamonds, set in a white-gold band.

FROM STUDENTS TO
Sweethearts

atherine Middleton waited a long time for her prince. The story of her romance with Prince William, from university days in Scotland, where they eventually shared a flat with friends, to gradual public appearances and cosy domesticity in out-of the-way cottages, is a slow-burning tale that has taken eight years to reach its denouement.

Catherine and William went up to St Andrews University in September 2001. They were billeted in the same hall of residence, St Salvator's, and they were both studying Art History. William remembered those days: 'We were friends for over a year first and it just sort of blossomed. We just spent more time with each other, had a good giggle, lots of fun, and realized we shared the same interests and had a really good time,' he said.

Catherine's memories of their first meeting are more personal: 'I actually think I went bright red and sort of scuttled off, feeling very shy,' she revealed.

There is no forgetting the Prince's reaction to Catherine's appearance in the annual charity fashion show at a St Andrews hotel, during their second term at university. He paid £200 for a front row seat and was bowled over

> Why did William wait so long to propose to the woman who is clearly the love of his life? He said that he knew the pressure of royal life was daunting and he wanted to give Catherine the opportunity to see 'what happens on the other side'. 'I wanted to give her the chance to see and to back out if she needed to, before it all got too much,' he said.

Right: Catherine was a guest at Prince William's graduation from Cranwell in April 2008, joining members of the Royal Family for the occasion.

Right: Catherine caught Prince William's eye when she modelled in a student fashion show at St Andrews in March 2002.

Far right: William is a keen polo player and here Catherine is at the Ham Polo Club, in Surrey, to watch him play.

when Catherine, who had become a friend, sashayed down the catwalk in a sheer shift dress. 'Wow!' was his reaction. The dress, designed by Charlotte Todd, was later sold at auction for thousands of pounds.

Although Catherine might have welcomed his attention, she already had a boyfriend and did not want to give the wrong impression. She wisely kept the attraction she and the young Prince were feeling for each other low key, and let matters develop slowly.

By the time they went up for their second year, they had become part of a group of four friends sharing a flat in the town, but still they managed to keep things discreet, never touching or holding hands in public, arriving at parties separately and, to the world and the sharp-eyed press, they were just good friends.

It was Catherine who persuaded Prince William not to give up his university course when, in the early days, he decided that Art History was not for him. She was instrumental in ensuring that he carried on studying, later switching his degree to Geography.

By the time William's 21st birthday was celebrated with a party at Windsor Castle in June 2003, it is likely that William and Catherine were romantically linked, although the Prince denied that he had a steady girlfriend.

After the Prince's proposal was accepted came the hardest part for the happy couple – keeping their good news secret for almost four weeks. Catherine gave back the ring for safe keeping and for a while she, her fiancé and her father, whose permission William had sought, were the only three people to know.

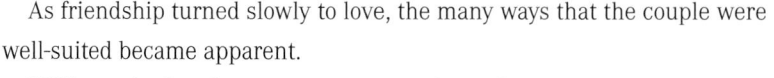

As friendship turned slowly to love, the many ways that the couple were well-suited became apparent.

William, the handsome young man who will one day be king, could have had his pick of European princesses and aristocratic young women for his bride. But his heart has been captured by an ordinary, although extraordinarily attractive, girl from the Home Counties.

This bodes well for the future, indicating that William is unpretentious and will listen to his own feelings rather than trying to satisfy convention.

In Catherine he has found a woman with whom he feels comfortable. She is sporty and shares his love of the outdoor life – a must for anyone joining the Royal Family – and is cheerful, resourceful, uncomplicated and creative.

They share a sense of humour: 'She's got a really naughty sense of humour, which kind of helps me, because I've got a really dry sense of humour. We had a good laugh – and things happened,' he said.

They were close enough during their third and final years at university to share a secluded cottage, establishing a cosy domesticity, but still managing to keep the relationship a secret. Their tight circle of friends helped, never breaking the code of silence that bound them to the young couple.

But once they left university that was impossible. William had to fulfil his royal duties and forge his career, the press never far away. By the time the pair had been spotted on the slopes enjoying a skiing holiday together at Klosters, Switzerland, the secret was out in the open. No one had seen them behaving like lovers, but they were often spotted together and suddenly, Catherine – who had just moved into a flat in central London with an old friend from her boarding-school days – found the full glare of the media spotlight on her private life.

She coped admirably, resigned to the fact that she would have to dress carefully, wear make-up and be suitably coiffured every time she stepped outside in order to face the photographers lying in wait.

Catherine kept a low profile at major events. She was not seen at the marriage of Prince Charles and Camilla Parker Bowles in 2005, although she did attend other weddings with William that year.

Left: Prince William takes part in the Sovereign's Parade at Sandhurst, in December 2006, as he passes out to receive his commission with the Household Cavalry in the Blues and Royals.

Since 2007 Catherine has appeared at a number of high-profile events, including the Princes' Concert for Diana, where she was a VIP guest in the royal box, and William's 'Wings' presentation ceremony in April 2008. She was also invited to the wedding of Peter Phillips, The Queen's grandson. This was the occasion where she first met The Queen. And in June 2008 she was asked to St George's Chapel, Windsor Castle, where she watched William's investiture into the Order of the Garter.

Above: Catherine Middleton, flanked by her father Michael and mother Carole, is an invited guest at Prince William's passing out parade at the Royal Military Academy, Sandhurst.

Far left: Prince William's grandmother, Queen Elizabeth II, inspects her grandson as he graduates as an army officer during the Sovereign's Parade at the Royal Military Academy, Sandhurst, in December 2006.

Left: Prince Charles, the Prince of Wales and Camilla, Duchess of Cornwall watch Prince William at his passing out ceremony as an army officer at Sandhurst.

Although William continued to deny that marriage was in the air, their relationship was widely accepted, especially after he was photographed kissing Catherine at another Klosters holiday in 2006. It seemed too that the Royal Family had accepted her as William's girlfriend when images of William and his father, happy and at ease in her company, were circulated in the press.

Pressure from William's life in the forces was blamed for the couple's brief separation in early spring 2007 – but within weeks they were back together again as if nothing had happened.

A TWENTY-FIRST-CENTURY Prince

Early in the morning of 23 June 1982, a young father stood proudly on the steps outside St Mary's Hospital, Paddington, tenderly holding his newborn baby son.

He was not allowed to leave quietly. Cameras flashed and whirred, while journalists and television crews shouted questions as Prince Charles, heir to the throne, held the child who would also one day be king.

But the then unnamed baby, just 36-hours old, who bore a tag on his tiny wrist identifying him only as 'Baby Wales', scarcely stirred, undisturbed by the commotion and public rejoicing at his arrival.

'The birth of our son has given us both more pleasure than you can imagine,' said a tired and delighted Prince. 'It has made me incredibly proud and somewhat amazed.'

Prince William Arthur Philip Louis of Wales entered the world at 9.03 p.m. on 21 June in the private Lindo Wing of St Mary's Hospital. He was driven home to Kensington Palace, where he was to spend the next 16 years of his life.

William's great-grandmother, the late Queen Elizabeth the Queen Mother, celebrated her birthday on 4 August and that was the date in 1982 chosen for the christening of the newest member of the Royal Family. The ceremony, in the Music Room of Buckingham Palace, was conducted by the then Archbishop of Canterbury, Dr Robert Runcie. Young William was dressed in the Royal Family's ancient Honiton lace christening gown, first worn by the future King Edward VII. The two-month old baby was baptized with water from the River Jordan, poured into the traditional Lily Font, used for every royal christening since 1840.

Left: Young William after his first day at nursery school, with a finger puppet he had made for his mother.

Prince William became the first 'heir presumptive' (an heir, other than the first in line to the throne) to be born in an ordinary hospital, albeit in an expensive private wing, rather than in a royal residence. This was seen by many as a sign that the young Prince was entering a changing world, far different from that occupied by his father in 1948.

Right: Prince William at the age of 19.

William's mother, Princess Diana, whose love for her children shone through all she did, was determined to be hands-on when it came to bringing up her children. From the start, she gave William the constant attention and affection all babies need. It was she who nicknamed him 'Wills' and later 'Wombat', two names that have stayed with him. Her first big test came just a few weeks after his birth when she and Prince Charles were due to leave Britain for a long tour of Australia. Those who assumed that Diana would leave her precious son behind, in the care of his nanny and the nursery staff, were more than surprised when the young mother insisted that her child should travel with her.

If traditionalists criticized her 'modern' approach to rearing the heir presumptive, the rest of the world did not. There was general approval as pictures were shown of William's nanny, Barbara Barnes, carrying the baby from the aircraft onto Australian soil as they landed on the other side of the world.

There was a surge of excitement outside a small private nursery school in Notting Hill Gate as the children arrived for the new term in September 1985. A crowd of reporters and photographers jostled for position, cameras trained on one small boy dressed in red shorts and a red check shirt.

It had been no easy decision to send William to nursery school: royal children were normally taught at home by a governess until they were at least seven years old. However, Diana was keen that her son should escape the hothouse atmosphere of the Palace and learn how to socialize with other children.

The transition from being the centre of attention of his nanny, Barbara Barnes, to one of many children at school was probably a hard lesson to learn, but it has stood William in good stead.

Just two years later he moved from nursery school to the pre-prep Wetherby, West London, where there was more scope for his obvious aptitude for sport and enjoyment in taking part in school activities. It was at this time that a new nanny, Ruth Wallace, arrived at Kensington Palace to teach her young charge not only self-reliance but also the importance of consideration and kindness to others.

Both William and later his younger brother Harry moved on to become boarders at Ludgrove School in Berkshire, where William excelled at sport. He was tall for his age and soon became captain of both the rugby and hockey teams, and one of the school stars at clay pigeon shooting, having learned how to handle a gun from a very early age. Another early lesson that every member of the Royal Family has to learn is that they are forever in the public eye. As eventual heir to the throne, William has had to understand that the job is one for life. During his childhood and as he grew up, he accompanied his parents on a number of official duties so that he could get used to the attention he will always receive.

He has inherited not only the Windsor sense of duty, but also his mother's easy manner with the crowds, and his own charisma and self-assurance stand him in good stead in all his public duties.

Above: Princes William and Harry and their cousin, Peter Phillips, play on a fire engine on the Sandringham Estate in Norfolk, in January 1988. The princes' mother, Princess Diana, is watching over them.

Above: William takes part in a race at a school sports day, in June 1988.

One of those first public engagements took place when, at just eight years old, he accompanied his parents on a visit to Llandaff Cathedral in 1991 to celebrate St David's Day. A visit to the principality from which William takes his title was an appropriate baptism into public life and he wore a bright yellow daffodil in his buttonhole. It was when the young Prince, under the watchful eye of his mother, signed his name in the visitors' book at the cathedral, that onlookers noticed that he was left-handed.

Far left: The Princess of Wales, holding Prince Harry by the hand and with William at her side, arrives at the Nottingham Medical Centre in September 1990, to visit Prince Charles, who was a patient at the hospital.

Left: William, wearing a daffodil, accompanies his parents on an official visit to Wales in 1991.

Below: William and Harry enjoy a boat trip with their mother, Princess Diana, at Niagara Falls in 1991.

For several years Princess Diana was the unofficial mascot of the Welsh rugby team and a fervent supporter, taking William and Harry with her to international matches. Both boys took pride in learning the words of the Welsh National anthem – in Welsh – so that they could join in the community singing.

Another break with royal tradition came when it was time for the young Prince to continue his education. The sometimes tough regime of Gordonstoun, the Scottish public school attended by William's grandfather, father and uncles, was eschewed in favour of Eton College, possibly the most famous educational establishment in the world. The Berkshire college, with its centuries-long tradition of producing self-confident young men, was a happy selection. It was the first choice of both Diana and the Queen Mother, while William was pleased, not only that many of his friends from Ludgrove would be with him, but also that the school was close to Windsor Castle where he could join his grandmother, The Queen, for Sunday tea.

'William Wales' signed the Eton schoolbook in September 1995, on his first day there. His study-bedroom, in Manor House (where he was the only boy afforded the luxury of a private bathroom), was a cell-like 4 metres (13 feet) by 3 metres (10 feet) with a narrow single bed. William stamped his own mark on it by putting up a picture of Aston Villa football team, a signed poster of All Saints (his favourite band) and various pin-up posters.

As at Ludgrove, William excelled at sports, enjoying football and rugby, and shone especially in the school pool where he became the 'Keeper of Swimming' – Eton-speak for captain of the swimming team.

He did well academically too, gaining three A-levels with grades good enough to win a place at St Andrews University. But first he decided to see something of the world by taking a gap year.

Travel, adventure and education were the criteria for the widening of William's education. His first destination was Belize, the former British Honduras in Central America, where he joined the Welsh Guards on exercise in the wet, stifling hot and humid jungle. He had to learn what to do if bitten by a snake (chop its head off and keep the body to assess the dose of venom received), and how to kill and gut chickens before cooking them over an open fire. It was here that he first used semi-automatic weapons.

Far left: Prince William during his first year at Eton.

Left: Prince William in action as he captains his team in a school football tournament between Eton houses Gaileys (the Prince's team) and Hursts.

Right: On his gap year in Chile, the Prince, against the backdrop of the Andes, walks to work in the village of Tortel.

Below: William wearing his patriotic 'Pop' waistcoat, a privilege of sixth-formers at Eton.

The distinctive Eton uniform of black tail coat, striped trousers, waistcoat and white bow tie was established in 1820, when the whole establishment went into mourning for the death of King George III. When William was elected a member of 'Pop', the elite group of sixth-formers at the college allowed to wear waistcoats of their own choice – the more startling the better – he enthusiastically took advantage of this privilege.

If the jungles of Belize were steamy and uncomfortable, the soft white sands, blue sea, warm sun and gentle breezes of Mauritius in the Indian Ocean were pure delight. One 'Brian Woods', aka 'William Wales', registered on the island of Rodrigues as a helper with the Royal Geographical Society's 'Shoals of Capricorn' programme on marine conservation.

Chile came next, during the cold, wet and miserable rainy season. The first week of this Raleigh International expedition saw torrential rain, day and night. The young volunteers, soaked to the skin, had never experienced anything like it.

'Eventually even the tent became wet through; it was saturated ... we became quite demoralized even though we somehow managed to keep ourselves going by singing, telling jokes and stories ...,' said William on his return. But, when the rain stopped, the volunteers moved to the village of Tortel, teaching English to the children and making friends with the locals.

Anyone seeing the two young sons of Diana, Princess of Wales walking slowly, heads bowed, behind her funeral cortège on 6 September 1997 could not have failed to be moved. The boys were at particularly vulnerable ages – William was 15 and his brother Harry just two years younger – when their beloved mother died in a tragic car accident in Paris.

Despite the public outpouring of grief, the young princes, whatever they were feeling inwardly, kept their emotions firmly under control, showing a maturity that belied their years.

William took on the mantle of older brother with particular care after Diana's death, giving the younger Harry the unqualified support that he may have needed.

The boys have found security at their father's home, Highgrove, Gloucestershire, with Prince Charles who coped admirably with their care after Princess Diana's death. The family circle now includes the Duchess of Cornwall, the former Camilla Parker Bowles, Charles's long-time companion and second wife.

Since William went away to school, first to Ludgrove and then to Eton, his domestic life has been one of contrasts. At home – Highgrove, St James's Palace in London, Balmoral in Scotland or Sandringham in Norfolk – he would be gently woken each morning by a footman bearing a 'calling tray' with his pot of coffee and biscuits. His curtains would be drawn, the radio turned on and clothes laid out by a valet, primed the night before of that day's activities. Breakfast included a 'full English' or a choice of cereals and fruit. William usually ate the latter.

Prince William, who changed his university subject from Art History to Geography, won a Scottish Master of Arts degree with upper second class honours – the highest university honours gained by an heir to the British throne.

Left: William, Harry and their father, Prince Charles, became a close-knit trio after the death of Princess Diana in August 1997.

Right: Prince Charles and his sons enjoy a skiing holiday in the Swiss resort Klosters in 2005.

There was no such luxury at Eton and there were certainly no servants to make the early morning routine go smoothly when, in September 2001, William Wales went up to St Andrews University in Scotland, joining the 6,000 other students who swell the population of the town during term-time.

At first he lived in the rambling Gothic hall of residence, St Salvator's Hall ('Sallies' to its inhabitants), where he tumbled out of bed in the morning, showered and helped himself to breakfast in the communal dining hall, sitting next to whoever happened to be there at the time. He usually opted for the healthy choice but just occasionally fell prey to a couple of bacon butties and a mug of tea.

Breakfast over and teeth brushed, he would join fellow students in the lecture rooms or see his tutor to discuss an essay or, if there was no work on the agenda, would stroll into town to buy the newspapers and perhaps join friends for a coffee.

It was at St Andrews that William met Catherine Middleton with whom he and two other friends eventually moved out of hall to share a flat.

William's grandmother, Her Majesty Queen Elizabeth II, laid down a few ground rules for William at university. These were: no smoking, only moderate drinking and certainly no drugs. If he dated a woman he was never to be seen kissing her in public. Nor was he ever to ask his bodyguard to leave him alone, even at private parties. The last was a rule that William had observed since he was old enough to understand the ways of the world: never to discuss any member of the Royal Family, even with those to whom he had become close.

On Remembrance Sunday 2010, just two days before the announcement of his engagement to Catherine Middleton and the media frenzy that the news provoked, William decided to pay his respects to the British troops risking their lives in Afghanistan. To the surprise of many he flew out to join the men and women in the front line, taking part in the Remembrance Day Service with them.

The future king has a strong sense of duty, instilled in him by his Windsor forebears. He also takes a keen interest in various charitable causes, many of them once supported by his mother, Princess Diana. He and his brother Harry were taken by their mother on visits to Centrepoint, the charity for young homeless people supported by Diana, and also to shelters and clinics for those suffering from HIV/AIDS. He took on patronage of Centrepoint and, to prove his commitment, William went so far as to sleep rough on a freezing December night near Blackfriars Bridge.

He and Harry helped raise £40,000 for survivors of the devastating Asian tsunami by playing in a charity polo match just days after the terrible event on Boxing Day 2004. A week later the brothers volunteered at a British Red Cross distribution centre, making up aid packages for those affected by the disaster.

Above: William shakes hands with the crowd at the BAFTA awards at the Royal Opera House, Covent Garden, London, in February 2010.

Above: Prince William visits HM Naval Base at Faslane, in Scotland, to present gold pins to submariners in October 2010.

Even at the age of 15, Prince William was aware of his mother's passion for charity work. He was pleased that the 2,000-strong congregation who attended her funeral service in Westminster Abbey had included representatives of the many organizations that she had helped and supported.

While on his gap year William clearly enjoyed working with young children in the southern Chilean village of Tortel, where he taught English at the school and helped with various building projects. Back in the UK he did a stint of work experience at the children's unit at the Royal Marsden Hospital and soon became a patron of the institution. He is also a patron of Mountain Rescue England and Wales, and of the African-based Tusk Trust which works to conserve wildlife, and help with community development and education across the vast continent. His first official duty with the charity was in 2007, when he launched a 5,000-mile (8,000-km) bike ride across Africa.

Sport is high on Prince William's agenda and it follows that he has become the figurehead of some sporting organizations, raising money for charity through activities such as polo. He has taken part in charity runs with teams from Sandhurst and Clarence House to boost the coffers of Sports Relief, and he is also patron of the English Schools' Swimming Association.

Since he was a schoolboy William has supported Aston Villa football team and in May 2006 he became President of England's Football Association. His grandmother, The Queen, is patron of the Welsh Rugby Union and the Prince is in effect her deputy, having been appointed vice royal patron of the Union.

Sometime in the future Prince William of Wales KG FRS will be crowned King William V. This is his destiny and every aspect of his life has been shaped with his role as sovereign the predominant factor.

With the kingship in prospect, William can never be too ambitious about a career or profession, nor will he ever know the struggle of having to make his own way in life. What he can do while he waits, as his father has done for several decades, is to further his military career and to become accustomed to the round of public duties and sponsorship of a variety of causes.

After leaving university William underwent work experience from land management to banking, but, in the best royal tradition, eventually settled on a career in the armed forces.

He graduated from Sandhurst in December 2006 after spending almost a year at the Royal Military Academy there, receiving his commission as a lieutenant and watched at the passing out parade by his proud father and his grandmother The Queen.

Left: Prince William, President of the English Football Association, is seen here with David Beckham and Prince Harry at a reception to mark the 2010 FIFA World Cup in June 2010, in Johannesburg, South Africa.

Below: In March 2011 William visited Australia on a tour of regions devastated by the floods and Hurricane Yasi. Here he meets residents of Cairns, Queensland. The Prince's trip followed a visit to the earthquake zone in Christchurch, New Zealand, where he attended a memorial service for victims of the earthquake.

During his secondment to RAF Cranwell, the Prince was part of the crew on a C-17 Globemaster sent to Afghanistan to bring back the body of a British serviceman who had been killed in action. William was known affectionately by his fellow airmen as 'Billy the Fish'.

'The one thing his father and I were absolutely agreed on was that William would have as normal an upbringing as possible,' said his mother Diana, Princess of Wales. But normality is difficult to achieve for a young man who is unable to make a move without informing his bodyguards and on whom the hopes of the monarchy are fixed. What William has done, probably more than any other member of the Royal Family, is to bridge the gap between the monarchy and the British people. His marriage to Catherine Middleton will strengthen that bridge.

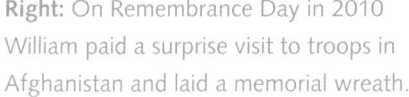

Right: On Remembrance Day in 2010 William paid a surprise visit to troops in Afghanistan and laid a memorial wreath.

Lieutenant William Wales followed his younger brother Harry into the Blues and Royals (the Household Cavalry Regiment) as a troop commander in an armoured reconnaissance unit.

His wish to see active service was discouraged, so William trained in both the Royal Navy and the Royal Air Force, winning commissions as sub-lieutenant in the former and flying officer in the latter.

An intensive four-month training course at Cranwell won him his RAF wings, presented to him in April 2008 by his father, a ceremony that was watched by, among others, Catherine Middleton.

A period with the Royal Navy followed, during which William, on board HMS *Iron Duke* in the Caribbean, took part in a secret underwater mission, helping to foil drug smugglers.

In February 2011 he received his first honorary army appointment, becoming a Colonel in the Irish Guards, a regiment of which his grandmother, The Queen, is Colonel-in-Chief.

Although William has been denied military service in combat zones, he was still able to be an active member of the armed services and, with this in mind, he trained to become a helicopter pilot with the RAF's Search and Rescue Force.

He is now based at RAF Valley on Anglesey, where he is expected to remain with No. 22 Squadron until 2013, working on board Sea King helicopters. His first rescue mission, as co-pilot in October 2010, was to an offshore gas rig in Morecambe Bay to airlift a sick man to hospital on the mainland.

A MODERN *Duchess*

Catherine Middleton, Britain's future Queen Catherine, knows that in marrying Prince William she has, in a way, married the whole nation. When he succeeds to the throne her husband will be subjected to an almost daily round of public duties, and she will be at his side.

Having been close to William for several years, Catherine must have some idea of the constant pressure they will both be under. William certainly does: on the day of their engagement he told the world that he had waited so long to ask her to be his wife in order to give her the chance to 'back out' of such an enormous commitment.

Catherine is, in royal parlance, 'a commoner', a middle-class woman from a wealthy self-made family with loving parents who have given her every advantage educationally and socially. She is well-mannered without being stuffy, charming without being precious, good-tempered and accommodating but with a will and mind of her own that will endear her to the British public.

Catherine's parents and siblings have already passed the 'loyalty test'. In the years that she and William have been together they have never let slip any details about the relationship. And, because she has had to behave as discreetly as a royal, her own family, especially her mother Carole and sister Pippa, have been an ever-present comfort, always ready with dependable support and advice.

Catherine Elizabeth Middleton was born at the Royal Berkshire Hospital, Reading, on 9 January 1982, making her just five months older than her fiancé.

On her mother's side Catherine is descended from a line of Durham miners. Her maternal grandfather, Ron Goldsmith, left school at 14 and eventually established a building business in Southall, West London. His daughter Carole, Catherine's mother, joined BOAC, the then international airline, as a stewardess and, during the 1970s, met and married Michael Middleton.

Mr Middleton had grown up in Leeds where his father, a pilot, came from forebears who were solicitors, mill owners and minor landowners. Michael, for a while a steward with BOAC, trained as a pilot before working in airline administration.

Christened 'Catherine' but known to the world until her marriage as 'Kate', Prince William's wife has indicated that she will use the more formal version of her name. On her husband's eventual succession to the throne she will become the sixth Queen Catherine, following Henry V's wife Catherine of Valois (d. 1437), three wives of Henry VIII, Catherine of Aragon (d. 1536), Catherine Howard (beheaded 1542) and Catherine Parr (d. 1548), and later, Catherine of Braganza who married Charles II in 1662.

It was after the birth of their third child, James, that Carole Middleton had the brainwave that would make the family fortune. She spotted a gap in the party market and set up a mail-order business selling costumes, toys, games and novelties for parties of all sorts.

By the time the business had expanded successfully, adapting well to the advent of the Internet, the Middletons – Carole and Michael with their three children Catherine, Pippa and James – were able to move into their large five-bedroom detached family house in the Berkshire village of Buckleberry.

Above: Catherine smiles as she visits the University of St Andrews in February 2011 with her fiancé, Prince William, to launch a fundraising campaign. The launch, at the university where the couple met, was one of their first official engagements together.

The success of the Middletons' family business, now run from a large barn at their Berkshire home, enabled Catherine's parents to give her a privileged education, sending her first to St Andrew's School in Pangbourne and then to Marlborough College, where she justified the £29,000 a year fees by becoming an admirable student academically, socially and on the sports field.

Marlborough College, founded in 1843 by the Church of England for the sons of impoverished clergy, is built around a pretty Queen Anne house on rolling Wiltshire downland and has educated some of Britain's most prominent women. Prime Minister's wife Samantha Cameron was educated there, as were Princess Eugenie of York, Emily Sheffield (deputy editor of *Vogue*), writers Frances Osborne and Lauren Child (creator of the Charlie and Lola books), model Stella Tennant and designer Antonia Robinson.

Friends who were at school with Catherine remember her as an initially shy girl who transformed into a confident outgoing teenager, hard-working, athletic and easy-going. She was described as popular, level-headed and talented. At Marlborough she met the children of the rich and famous but, like all Marlburiennes, she learnt how to be fair and tough. Marlborough girls have the reputation of being polite without being bland, thoughtful without appearing too earnest, and thoroughly civilized.

Poet John Betjeman was a pupil at Marlborough College and loathed it – 'Doom, Shivering doom! Inexorable bells to early school,' he wrote. Maybe he would have liked it better if girls, who were first admitted to the sixth form in 1968, had been there in his day.

Left: Catherine enjoys a day out at the horse trials at Gatcombe Park, in Gloucestershire, in August 2005.

Right: Catherine graduates from St Andrews University, in June 2005.

Above: Catherine takes part in a training session for a charity rowing event, in June 2007.

Above: Prince William and Catherine take a ski lift at Klosters, Switzerland, in March 2008.

Catherine, who achieved three good A-levels, including A grades for Maths and Art, discovered that you could not be a shrinking violet or take yourself too seriously at the college. But she did find the freedom to discover herself and not worry about what others might think. The girls were not expected to be brilliant, but they had to join in. Many of her fellow pupils were unconventional but most were passionate about something, whether it was writing, painting, history, science or music.

Catherine became head of her house, Elmhurst, where she is still remembered as being very good at mucking in, playing games – she was captain of the school hockey team – and acting. She was also known for her dependability and loyalty; all the qualities, in fact, for a perfect modern princess.

Like Prince William, Catherine opted for a gap year before going on to St Andrews University to study Art History. And, like William, she spent time working on a project in Chile, also visiting the Caribbean and Florence.

By the time Catherine arrived at Marlborough, once a boys-only college, girls were a fixture, but when the first female students were admitted in 1968 the prospect of being watched and 'marked' by dozens of boys was a daunting one. But it was character-forming. 'Anything after walking across court for the first time, watched by all those boys, is a piece of cake,' said one former pupil.

When Catherine Middleton went up to St Andrews University in the small Scottish town of the same name, she was not the only pupil there from her school, Marlborough College. Some of her former schoolmates knew Prince William, so it was not long before he and Catherine were on friendly terms – although she admits she felt embarrassed when they were first introduced.

But that embarrassment was quickly overcome. By the end of freshers' week Catherine had been dubbed the prettiest girl at 'Sallies' (St Salvator's Hall) and both she and the Prince were enrolled on the same course. Soon they were meeting over the breakfast muesli and fruit, served in the grand ground-floor dining hall with the light filtering through its stained-glass windows, portraits of Scottish philosophers lined up above them on the walls.

They had a love of the countryside, sporting pursuits and swimming in common. By coincidence their gap years had followed a similar pattern and Catherine was able to talk about the Renaissance art she had seen in Florence and which would be figuring on the Art History course.

But talking was all that happened at this stage. They both had romantic liaisons with other people during their first term and when William came to realiize that he was not enjoying his course, finding the workload challenging, there was serious talking to be done. A decision to switch to a Geography course and a growing interest in the pretty chestnut-haired student, who seemed quieter and more sympathetic than many of the others, did the trick.

At the beginning of their second year William and Catherine, with two other friends, moved into a property in Hope Street in St Andrews town centre. This was fitted out like no other student accommodation, with bullet-proof windows, bomb-proof doors and a sophisticated laser security system. Here they entertained friends, threw dinner parties and allowed their romance to blossom.

Through all this, Catherine was discretion itself. She was careful not to be seen in any compromising situation with William and it was not until they were photographed making their way together up the slopes on a ski lift at Klosters, in June 2004, that anyone outside their close-knit circle of friends had any inkling that they were romantically linked.

University friends remember that, although Catherine had become the girlfriend of the most eligible man at university, she never boasted or gloated. And, most importantly, she always followed the unwavering royal rule of never talking about their relationship.

St Andrews has a reputation as a university for forging long-lasting relationships. At William and Catherine's graduation ceremony in June 2005, the university's vice-chancellor Dr Brian Lang uttered words that many have seen as prophetic: 'You will have made lifelong friends,' he told the young people seated in front of him. 'You may have met your husband or wife. Our title as the top match-making university in Britain signifies so much that is good about St Andrews, so we rely on you to go forth and multiply.'

Above: Prince William and his fiancée launch a fundraising campaign at their old university, St Andrews, in February 2011.

57

Catherine graduated from St Andrews University with a good degree in Art History, but she decided to make a career in the fashion business, for a while becoming an accessories buyer for the high street clothes chain Jigsaw.

But her parents' successful family company, selling partyware of all kinds, needed a marketing manager, so in 2007 she decided to work at promoting the business back home in rural Berkshire.

That all had to stop when she became William's fiancée. She handed over projects such as designing the Christmas catalogue, arranging press coverage for the thriving company, organizing photo shoots and visiting trade fairs to others; suddenly her job was to become a member of the Royal Family.

Many royal marriages are arranged to unite two nations, or as a marriage of convenience between two families eager to strengthen their ties by such a union. This marriage is different. Catherine and William are the prime movers and it is they who have made decisions on their own terms calmly and soberly. It is clear that they have married for love, and with a great deal of friendship and goodwill on both sides.

Catherine comes from a warm and happy family who have welcomed Prince William into their home without fuss or pretension, never boasting to the neighbours or letting slip details about the relationship to the media. That discretion, and Catherine's own loyalty and quiet perseverance, has stood her in good stead, winning the approval of her grandmother-in-law, The Queen.

Catherine has been discreet, too, about past relationships. We know that in her first term at university she dated Rupert Finch, a talented cricketer and now a lawyer, but neither he nor she has ever spoken about their friendship.

Left: William and Catherine undertake their first official engagement together as they launch a new lifeboat at Trearddur Bay, Anglesey, in North Wales, in February 2011.

Above: William and Catherine visit the New Zealand High Commission in London to sign the book of condolence in memory of those who lost their lives in the New Zealand earthquake in February 2011.

Above: The couple enjoy a surprise visit to Belfast, Northern Ireland, on Shrove Tuesday 2011. They both had a successful go at pancake-tossing during a street celebration of Pancake Day.

Like William she enjoys partying but, even during their brief break-up in 2007, her name has never been linked to that of any other serious boyfriend.

Patience is another virtue and Catherine has displayed that quality over the years when she and William were playing the waiting game. During the many times that William has been away on royal duties, family holidays or undergoing his periods of training and service with the armed forces, Catherine has shown that she was prepared to stay at home without fuss and with the stoicism she will need to display for the rest of her life.

These qualities – her innate sense of discretion, the self-containment she has displayed throughout the relationship, and her good-humoured patience and resilience – have been noted by her in-laws, who have clearly given Catherine the royal seal of approval.

59

CATHERINE'S *Style*

P rince William could not help but notice when 'quiet Kate', the girl he had enjoyed chatting to at breakfast in the university dining hall, sashayed down the catwalk, looking spectacular in a dramatic black dress. But something so exotic, worn to raise money for charity, is not Catherine's normal style.

At university she was happy to wear the student 'uniform' of jeans, sweaters and jackets – the warmer the better, to cope with the bracing Scottish climate.

Catherine is tall and slim, with long, glossy, deep-chestnut hair which she likes to wear loose and which suits her that way.

So she has adopted a refreshingly natural look which has won her several fashion accolades, including a listing in the top ten *Tatler* style icons, the 'most promising newcomer' award in a *Daily Telegraph* list of style winners and a place in *Vanity Fair*'s international best-dressed list.

Catherine knows she has a lot to live up to: William's mother, the late Princess Diana, was an international style icon. But Catherine's great strength is that she wears fashion in the same way as other women of her age but with a quiet grace and an easy manner that makes the simplest outfit stylish and stunning. Everyone can relate to her unfussy style.

Copies of Catherine's sophisticated knee-length sapphire blue silk-jersey wrap dress by designer Issa sold out within hours of the announcement of her engagement to Prince William. Her stunning ivory lace and satin wedding dress, designed by Sarah Burton of British fashion house Alexander McQueen, was also copied by dressmakers around the world and on sale just days after the wedding.

Right: Catherine at the wedding of William's close friend Nicholas van Cutsem to Alice Hadden-Paton at The Guards Chapel, Wellington Barracks, London, in August 2009.

Far left: Catherine models designer knitwear at a student fashion show in St Andrews.

Centre: Warm as toast in a fur hat, Catherine braves the March winds to attend the Cheltenham Gold Cup.

Left: Catherine's hat was a conversation piece at the wedding of William's stepsister, Laura Parker Bowles, at Lacock, in Wiltshire, in 2006.

Her post-university style of jeans or casual trousers tucked into long leather boots and teamed with a blouse and jacket looked good. For the short while that she worked for high street fashion house Jigsaw she was to be spotted wearing their clothes, along with other stylish brands such as L.K. Bennett, Kew and Whistles.

But latterly her tastes have become more up-market and sophisticated. She is clearly supporting British fashion designers and brands, which is good news for the home-grown fashion market for whom she will become an ambassador. The silk-jersey dress that she wore to announce her engagement was by Issa, a British company owned and run by Daniella Issa Helayel. Her wedding dress was from one of the most well-known British fashion houses – Alexander McQueen – where Sarah Burton came up with a flawless elegant and classic design which suited Catherine perfectly.

Catherine goes for clear, bright colours that display her dark good looks to perfection. Reds, deep pinks and classic navy all look good on the new Duchess, tailored into clinging dresses, scoop neck blouses and tops, and well-cut trousers that show off her slim figure. Tailored jackets, nipped in to her waist, are a favourite, teamed with casual trousers, scarves and hats for a chic city-girl-about-town look.

Right: A chic outfit for the wedding of Hugh van Cutsem to Rose Astor, at Burford, in Oxfordshire, in June 2005.

Far right: Catherine wears a beret with style at the Cheltenham Festival in 2007.

A FUTURE Together

Good wishes for William and Catherine ride hand-in-hand with high hopes for the future of the British monarchy. Between them it is hoped that they will secure the long-term future of a monarchy which is in the process of modernization. It is already clear that they take their positions as future King and Queen Consort seriously.

Their first official engagements together began in February 2011 when they named a new lifeboat in Anglesey, in North Wales, where Prince William is based as an RAF helicopter pilot. The following day they travelled to St Andrews University, where they first met nine years ago. There they marked the Prince's appointment as patron of the university's 600th anniversary appeal. On Shrove Tuesday, 3 March, the couple made an official visit to Northern Ireland.

Throughout their married life The Duke and Duchess of Cambridge will be expected to represent the British monarchy overseas. Their first such trip comes at the beginning of July 2011 when they will visit Canada for eight days, travelling to Alberta, the Northwest Territories, Prince Edward Island, Quebec and Ottawa. The Princess knows that all eyes will be upon her and it is believed she has agreed to undertake at least one solo engagement.

Stephen Harper, the Canadian Prime Minister, who invited the young couple, expressed his delight: 'It is my sincere hope that their tour will be the start of a lasting relationship with Canada by the royal couple.' Prince William said he is keen to show his wife a country close to his family's heart.

Catherine and William will want to enjoy a period of cosy domesticity now that they are married. William's job, as a Search and Rescue helicopter pilot with No. 22 Squadron, is based at RAF Valley on the island of Anglesey. There the couple already have a cottage tucked away down a remote winding lane, where they will live when not undertaking official engagements. But, unlike most newly-weds, the pair will be given a London apartment and will have the pick of royal homes to visit throughout the year.

Family life is important to both William and Catherine. He is probably the first senior member of the Royal Family to have spent time with ordinary people in a way that those of his father's generation could not, and he has shown himself able to relax and enjoy the company of those around him.

The Prince is comfortable with his wife's parents, Carole and Michael, and has spent a considerable amount of time at their Berkshire home. The young couple will continue to be welcome visitors now that they are married.

They have both had time to get to know each other's families and it is clear that William's father and grandmother know that this union between middle England and a monarchy striving to be more modern is an excellent one.

Above: The couple share a smile during their official visit to the St Andrews University in February 2011.

ACKNOWLEDGEMENTS

The coats of arms on the inside front cover and the inside back cover are reproduced by kind permission of the College of Arms and Michael Middleton.

All photographs by kind permission of **Getty Images** except for: **Alamy**: 40 42br (Trinity Mirror/Mirrorpix), 41 (Allstar Picture Library), 43tr (Jayne Fincher Photo Int), 46 (Terry Fincher Photo Int), 61ct (Trinity Mirror); **Rex Features**: 37tr, 48br (Tim Rooke), 51, 61bc; **Pitkin Publishing**: 15 (Heather Hook); **Press Association**: 33 35 main (Kirsty Wigglesworth), inside back cover b; **Mark Slade:** 29b.